THIS JOURNAL BELONGS TO:

MW00886277